I0802379

IMAGES
of Rail

RHODE ISLAND TROLLEYS

On the Cover: Trolley Cars Nos. 680 and 1325. Throughout the years, the Buttonwoods line, with its many stations, was one of the busiest routes of the United Electric Railways (UER). Several trolley cars provided daily service to those living and working along the way. Turnouts were constructed along many routes, allowing cars to be diverted off of the main line and giving express cars the ability to pass, which improved travel times. (Courtesy of the authors.)

IMAGES
of Rail

RHODE ISLAND TROLLEYS

Joseph and Janice Soares

ARCADIA
PUBLISHING

ISBN 978-1-4671-2974-9

Published by Arcadia Publishing
Charleston, South Carolina

Printed in the United States of America

Library of Congress Control Number: 2018937813

For all general information, please contact Arcadia Publishing:
Telephone 843-853-2070
Fax 843-853-0044
E-mail sales@arcadiapublishing.com
For customer service and orders:
Toll-Free 1-888-313-2665

Visit us on the Internet at www.arcadiapublishing.com

We would like to dedicate this book to Francis Soares, who has provided valuable insight into the heyday of the trolley system in Rhode Island.

CONTENTS

Acknowledgments

While in our early 20s, we became interested in all things railroad. Our focus narrowed over time to trolleys. Being native Rhode Islanders, we began collecting old Rhode Island trolley photographs. It was our good fortune that this love of the trolley was also shared by many other wonderful people who graciously sold or shared many old photographs and images with us. We would like to thank those listed here for their efforts in preserving Rhode Island's trolley and railroad history: Larry Bass, Richard Wonson, Bob Suppicich, Stephen Boothroyd, and the Branford Electric Railway Association.

We would also like to thank the University of Rhode Island, Providence Public Library, the Rhode Island Public Transit Authority (RIPTA), the Rhode Island Historical Society, and the *Providence Journal*. Their assistance in this project was invaluable.

All images appear courtesy of the authors.

Introduction

Many of the first forms of public transportation, such as horse-drawn carriages and trolleys, began serving a small segment of the population in post–Revolutionary War America.

The history of Rhode Island's streetcar past is often confusing and not easily understood.

During the early years, Rhode Island had as many as 15 separate streetcar companies. Many of these companies, due to financial reasons or government regulations, leased, sold, or merged with other companies, making it difficult to easily distinguish one company from another. The complexity of this, along with other issues, makes the study of Rhode Island's streetcar history a fascinating endeavor. At its pinnacle, Rhode Island had over 320 miles of urban and suburban track, with Providence forming the nucleus. From Providence, one could travel by rail in many directions, including on interurban lines running to points in Massachusetts and Connecticut.

Here in Rhode Island, horse-drawn transportation took root early. During the end of the Civil War, the Providence and Pawtucket trolley lines began.

The apparent success of these lines encouraged many investors seeking to capitalize on this needed service; they began negotiating with the state and towns to obtain charters for other horse-drawn routes.

Within a few years, several horsecar companies, as they were called, took root, operating lines in Providence and surrounding areas.

Many early horse-drawn lines followed the old stagecoach routes. Many of these routes were widened and improved to accommodate the laying of track.

During the Civil War era, horse-drawn transportation began to prosper. It was in the country's small towns and cities where the roots of our modern mass transportation network began.

In January 1865, the Rhode Island General Assembly drafted legislation to unite several previously established horse-trolley companies under one name: the Union Railroad Company. The consolidation of several companies was intended to facilitate an ever-growing demand for new charters to be granted and the expansion of new trolley lines throughout the state.

This new company, named the Union Railroad Company, was adopted for the public good. This gave the company the ability to keep up with the ever-expanding transportation needs throughout the state. The company was encouraged by state officials to lay new track and purchase additional rolling stock to accommodate the state's rapidly growing transportation needs.

The history of the street railway in Rhode Island was similar to that of many other cities in the United States. The evolution from horse-drawn trolley cars to the electrification of the system took many years.

After the first introduction of the electric trolley in Rhode Island in 1889, ridership surged, reaching 24 million in 1892.

In 1893, the United Traction and Electric Company was formed by Nelson W. Aldrich, Marsden J. Perry, and William G. Roelker. This new company was made up of holdings of the Union Railroad Company and the Pawtucket Street Railway Company.

In 1902, out-of-state investors became interested in the United Traction and Electric Company. That year, they formed the Rhode Island Company, which was made up of leased United Traction holdings.

In 1913, the Rhode Island Company had 985 passenger cars, with 435 of them being the open type. A large number of these open cars were utilized during the summer months.

In its heyday, the Rhode Island Company was one of the largest trolley line systems in the United States. The company's track spanned nearly the entire state.

The New York, New Haven & Hartford Railroad, controlled by, J.P. Morgan and with Charles Mellen as president, began a relentless pursuit of acquiring smaller independent railroads, steamship lines, and trolley line companies in Rhode Island, Massachusetts, and Connecticut. They feared competition from these smaller transportation companies would cut into their profits.

Morgan and Mellen had a dream of acquiring the majority of transportation along the Southern New England coast from New York, Fall River, and Boston and putting it under their control. After Morgan and Mellen bought a controlling interest, the Rhode Island Company came under their control, along with other street railway companies.

The federal courts eventually ruled this to be a monopoly violating the Sherman Antitrust Act. A ruling was given that instructed the company to divest itself of a large portion of its transportation business interests, including street railways. The Rhode Island Company then came under the control of a federal trustee who, in 1919, petitioned the company into receivership. Shortly after the company was put into the hands of the appointed receivers, a strike broke out, initiated by the Street Carmen's Union, against the Rhode Island Company. The strike started on July 19, 1919. For 19 days, a transportation gridlock took hold.

The situation leading up to the strike had been heating up for some time. On the morning of the first day of the strike, many people found themselves unable to get to work. Many had to turn to other means of transportation. A number of local mills began providing transportation for their employees. Others arrived at work by horse and wagon or automobile.

The strike was centered around an increase in wages. At the beginning of the strike, the railway companies locked up their many car houses and equipment throughout the state. Negotiations between the railway companies and the strikers carried on for days and nights. After 19 days, an agreement was reached, and the strike was officially over.

After the Rhode Island Company was placed in receivership in 1919, two years of negotiations and court proceedings took place. The result was the formation of the United Electric Railways Company. This new company, made up of assets of the old Rhode Island Company and the United Traction and Electric Company, was vital to Rhode Island's economic health but had many obstacles to overcome.

One

The Patchwork of Companies and the Rhode Island Company

No. 8 at Elmwood Car Barn, c. 1911. Before the horse-drawn trolley, the horse-drawn stagecoach was the primary means of transportation for many in Rhode Island's small towns and cities. The main complaint regarding the horse-drawn stagecoach was the dirt and dust dredged up from the road surface in the summer months and muddy conditions during the rainy season. In addition, many roads were not maintained and became hazardous for drivers and passengers.

Market Square, Providence. In Rhode Island, the solution to hazardous road conditions came in 1865 with the laying of track on which a horse-drawn car could be pulled. The first track was laid out in Providence and ran from Market Square into Olneyville. Many in the city looked on eagerly as the road was torn up and the track was laid.

Mount Pleasant Car No. 256. The move to a track system was a great improvement. Even though the primary source of power was the horse, the riding conditions for the passengers and driver were greatly improved. The word of a better ride quickly spread, and ridership rapidly increased. This improvement also cut down on the wear and tear on the stagecoach car.

OLNEYVILLE (ABOVE) AND PAY CAR NO. 1500 ON SCRAP LINE (BELOW). The Cranston Railroad Company was granted permission to lay rails on several streets in Providence by the City of Providence in August 1864. Just a year prior, the city adopted an ordinance permitting the Providence, Pawtucket & Central Falls Railroad to put down track on certain roads in the city. Also adopted by the city council was an ordinance allowing a railroad company to use the track of another railroad company when necessary. Compensation for this use would need to be agreed upon prior to such use.

Car No. 1520 on Scrap Line (above) and Car No. 1858 (below). The Broadway & Providence Railroad Company, the South Main Street Horse Railroad Company, the Providence and Pawtucket Horse Railroad Company, and the Elmwood Horse Railroad Company were each given permission by the City of Providence in November 1964 to begin the installation of rails in the city of Providence. An annual payment for the right to operate within the city was a requirement accepted by the railroad companies.

No. 61 Elmwood, Reservoir and Butler Avenues. On November 28, 1864, the City of Providence adopted an ordinance permitting the Broadway & Providence Railroad Company, the South Main Street Horse Railroad Company, and the Elmwood Horse Railroad Company to lay rails in the city of Providence. Many people living in the city were happy to see the improvements the trolley companies made to the road surface. At the end of 1864, negotiations that would take the patchwork of Rhode Island horse lines and consolidate them into one company were in progress.

Seaview Station, Narragansett Pier. In 1904, there were 15 streetcar companies that held charters and operated in the State of Rhode Island. Of the 15 companies, 10 of them were controlled by the Rhode Island Company. One of these 10 was the Seaview Railroad.

Elmwood Car No. 618. Among the combined 15 companies, there were 836 trolley cars in service, with an additional 45 freight cars and 56 utility cars in use.

Ex-Horsecar, S. Auburn Scrap Line. Passenger safety was a top priority for electric railway companies. Accidents and mishaps were daily occurrences. Accidents that occurred in connection with the operation of trolley cars included mostly collisions and step accidents. The various trolley car houses kept daily records of accidents that occurred along the routes.

Rush Hour in Providence. Safety contests were routinely conducted by the United Electric Railways. These contests were competitions between the different trolley car houses situated throughout the state. The car house staff with the lowest number of accidents in a given time period won the contest and was treated to a dinner and other awards. These safety campaigns were quite effective.

Car No. 133, Rocky Point. Many of the first horse-drawn trolley cars in Rhode Island were somewhat unpleasant to look at due to their design. Over the years, improvements were made, and an overall standard design was adopted. The open, benched horsecar design became very popular.

Rocky Point Car at Grants Station. The open car—or "bloomer," as it was called—was much appreciated by most passengers in good weather. However, during cold weather, it made the ride much less enjoyable.

SUBURBAN CAR NO. 679 (ABOVE) AND SUBURBAN CRASH (BELOW), JUNE 1900. Suburban car No. 679, pictured above, was one of two Suburban cars involved in a head-on collision on June 10, 1900. It was regarded as one of the worst trolley car accidents in Rhode Island. The accident occurred on a curve just south of Warwick Station. The accident claimed six lives, with many other people left seriously injured.

CAR NO. 950, THE RHODE ISLAND COMPANY. In the summer of 1890, the Union Railroad Company did a study on converting from horse-drawn cars to electric. An electrified trolley line was put in place on the company's Broad Street route. The apparent success motivated the company to seek permission from the City of Providence to begin electrifying the entire system.

WASHINGTON MALL, NEWPORT. There are several noticeable events that stand out for making an indelible mark on Rhode Island's streetcar history. Within two years, from 1892 through 1894, the Union Railroad Company, seeing the clear benefit of the electric trolley car, converted most of its lines to be powered by electricity. The first line converted was in Providence in January 1892, and the conversion of the rest of the lines soon followed.

Watering Car, Providence. Water-sprinkling cars were basically motorized flatcars with a water tank mounted on them. The tank's capacity ranged from 1,500 to 5,000 gallons. Many tanks on the earlier cars were made of wood, much like a giant wooden barrel. Over time, the tanks were constructed of steel. Watering cars were used to control dust along the roadbed. At times, weed killer was added to the water to control grass and weeds growing around the tracks.

Auburn and Eden Park Car. In the early part of 1918, Providence was experiencing a municipal water shortage. The Rhode Island Company offered the use of its 4,000-gallon watering car to relieve the city's water shortage. The city much appreciated the offer during their time of distress but graciously declined.

Crossing Rocky Point Junction Station (above) and Duby's Grove Station (below), c. 1933. In Providence, traffic congestion was a constant concern for the trolley lines. The downtown loading district of Providence extended from Market Square to the east to Cathedral Square and Hoyle Square to the west and from Union Station to the Providence River in the other direction. Exchange Place, the city hall, and the post office were also highly congested. Between these points, as many as 65 to 75 trolley cars would run per hour. Over the years, different traffic patterns and track layouts were implemented in a constant effort to improve safety and efficiency.

Hoxsie Station. The installation of electric track signal switches at various points was one improvement made to increase traffic movement.

Car No. 670 at Buttonwoods Station. Along most trolley lines, stations were erected for the convenience of passengers waiting for a trolley. Selected locations along the route were marked by a white pole indicating where passengers could catch the trolley. In the early 1900s, there were numerous white-pole stops along most trolley routes. In 1913, 30 percent of the white-pole stops were removed, greatly increasing the track time on most routes.

Rocky Point, Broad Street Car (above), and Palace Gardens Station, Warwick (below). A terrible trolley accident occurred on a return trip from Crescent Park on the evening of June 3, 1906. Eleven people were killed and forty were injured when a trolley car they were in overturned in East Providence. The motorman driving the car was unfamiliar with the route and entered a curve at excessive speed, overturning the car. At the time of the accident, a heavy fog hung over the tracks, which contributed to the cause of the accident.

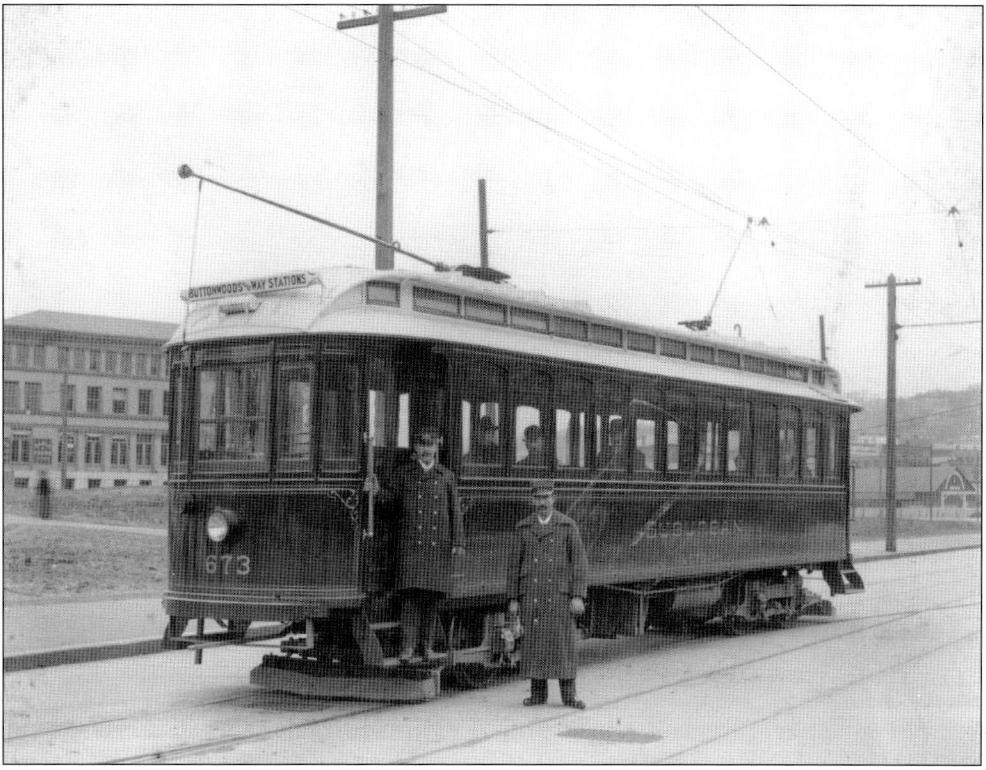

SUBURBAN CAR NO. 673 (ABOVE) AND PASCOAG TROLLEY CAR NO. 1759 (BELOW). In January 1900, the Rhode Island Suburban Railway Company had 36 trolley cars in service, with 20 of them heated by electric heaters. The average fare was 5¢. The Rhode Island Suburban Railway Company was controlled by the Rhode Island Company at this time. Suburban cars Nos. 673 and 679 ran on the Buttonwoods and Way Stations route.

Newport Street Railway Car No. 33 (above) and Olneyville Car (below). On January 1, 1901, the Newport Street Railway Company had 13 trolley cars in service, with 6 of them heated by electric heaters. The company had four utility cars that serviced the company's 4.7 miles of track. The company employed 25 people and charged its riders a fare of 5¢ per mile traveled.

Two

The United Electric Railways

Broad Street Car House. The life expectancy of a trolley car purchased in 1940 was about 17 years. Maintenance of a car in daily service was a top priority at all car houses. The Broad Street Car House had equipment and personnel that could quickly repair a disabled car, keeping the necessary number of cars in service and on time.

Jitney Bus at Eddy Street Terminal. In 1922, transportation and the way Rhode Islanders utilized it began to change. Rubber-tired vehicles, such as the jitney, began showing up throughout the state. This new manner of transportation began cutting into the profits of the electric railway companies.

First United Electric Railways Bus. A war for ridership began, with the United Electric Railways Company (UER) winning. A bill introduced by the governor in 1922 put control of jitneys in the hands of the public utilities commission. Before long, the commission transferred the jitney business to UER.

JITNEY 61 AT ROGER WILLIAMS PARK (ABOVE) AND NEW UNITED ELECTRIC RAILWAYS BUS (BELOW), C. 1922. The transfer of control of the jitney business to the public utilities commission temporarily helped United Electric Railways (UER), but by the 1930s, the taxi business and private automobiles whittled down UER profits to a point at which the company began threatening to close down many lines. Within a short time, and much like what happened with the jitney, the Rhode Island General Assembly placed taxis under the control of the public utilities commission.

No. 1703 on Chapin Avenue, Providence. The Woonsocket Street Railway Company was incorporated by the Rhode Island General Assembly in 1886. The company started out as a horse-drawn trolley company with less than five miles of track and two horsecars in service. In Woonsocket, after only a week of operating horse-drawn trolleys, the company began to experiment with the electrification of the trolley.

Woonsocket Car No. 63. Within days, a network of wires was strung along the route. On September 25, 1887, the power was turned on, and an electric car began to roll along South Main Street. A crowd of spectators had gathered to watch this amazing sight. At one spot along the way, the car derailed, but many willing hands pushed the car back onto the rails. The car continued up Globe Hill with the crowd cheering for it. The news of this electric trolley spread, with many seeking a ride on the new amusement.

TROLLEY CAR NO. 1511 ON A STREET (ABOVE) AND AT BROAD STREET CAR BARN (BELOW), C. 1948. The 1887 electrification experiment in Woonsocket foretold what future transportation might look like. By the end of 1887, the experiment ended in Woonsocket, and a return to horse-drawn trolleys resumed. Within years, electric trolleys were reintroduced, and by 1893, the whole line was electrified.

Providence & Danielson (P&D) Car No. 1512. This line ran from Market Square in Providence to Danielson, Connecticut. The line opened in the early part of the 1900s. It was 27.5 miles to the state line and another 7.5 miles to Danielson. The rolling stock consisted of eight boxcars and two combination cars. Over the years, many additional cars were added to the line. This line was very long and traveled through what was then a lightly populated area. These factors made the line unprofitable. However, it was important to the economy of Rhode Island.

Car No. 1512, Providence. This car came under the control of the Rhode Island Company in 1911. Many Providence & Danielson Railway cars not being used on the P&D line were brought to Providence and renumbered; P&D car No. 8 was renumbered 1512.

Westerly and Watch Hill Trolley. The Norwich & Westerly Railway Company operated a 21-mile line. It was first chartered as the Norwich, Mystic & Westerly Street Railway Company in 1903. After some changes to the route, it was renamed the Norwich & Westerly Railway Company in December 1905.

Steam Rail Puller, Elmwood Avenue. In 1893, the Pawcatuck Valley Street Railway was chartered by the Rhode Island General Assembly to build a line from the New Haven Railroad depot at Westerly to the seashore at Watch Hill. This line was just over six miles long. The route ran from Canal Street (near the Westerly Depot) to High Street, Dixon Square, through Broad and Main Streets, Beach Street, Thompson's Corner, and then on to Watch Hill.

NORWICH & WESTERLY CAR NO. 105. A summer trip on the Pawcatuck Valley Street Railway provided a 30-minute ride between Westerly and Watch Hill, with a fare costing 10¢. The company had eight trolley cars in 1899. Six of these were open cars, providing passengers with a cool breeze during the summer months. Due to several reasons, the Norwich & Westerly Railway became unprofitable, and in 1909, the company merged with the Pawcatuck Valley Street Railway.

BUILDER'S PHOTOGRAPH, NEW CAR NO. 1480. Over several years, the Norwich & Westerly Railway expanded its line, and by 1916, it was acquired by the Shore Line Electric Railway Company, which operated more than 59 miles of track consisting of the Norwich & Westerly, Pawcatuck Valley Street Railway, Ashaway & Westerly Railway, and Groton & Stonington Street Railway Companies.

Wickford, Narragansett Pier, and Wakefield Trolley (above); and East Greenwich, Car No. 1322 (below). The Narragansett Pier and Wakefield line was originally built by the Seaview Railroad and eventually came under the control of the Rhode Island Company. The line was constructed on a private right of way from East Greenwich to Wickford and then on to Narragansett Pier and Wakefield. Much like the Danielson line, the East Greenwich to Wickford line made its way through a lightly settled rural route, making it unprofitable. The Seaview line was about 19 miles long; the line was abandoned by the early 1920s.

Trolley No. 1323 on Pawtuxet River Bridge. The Pawtuxet Valley Electric Street Railway Company built a line to the Pawtuxet Valley villages of Hope, Clyde, Washington, and Crompton. The Rhode Island Suburban Railroad later took control of the line and extended it into Providence.

Derailment at Central Avenue, Pawtuxet. All too often, trolley cars jumped their tracks, causing many injuries and deaths. These derailments could be caused by collisions with other vehicles or a broken or faulty rail. In some cases, a failure of a trolley car wheel was to blame.

Builder's Photograph, Car No. 82. When a new trolley car was needed, the company would have a car manufacturer make a car for the needed purpose. Specifications for the type of car and other requirements were noted, and the manufacturers began building the car. When the car was at a certain stage or finished, a "builder's photograph" was taken and presented to the purchaser. The photograph shows a basic overview of the built car.

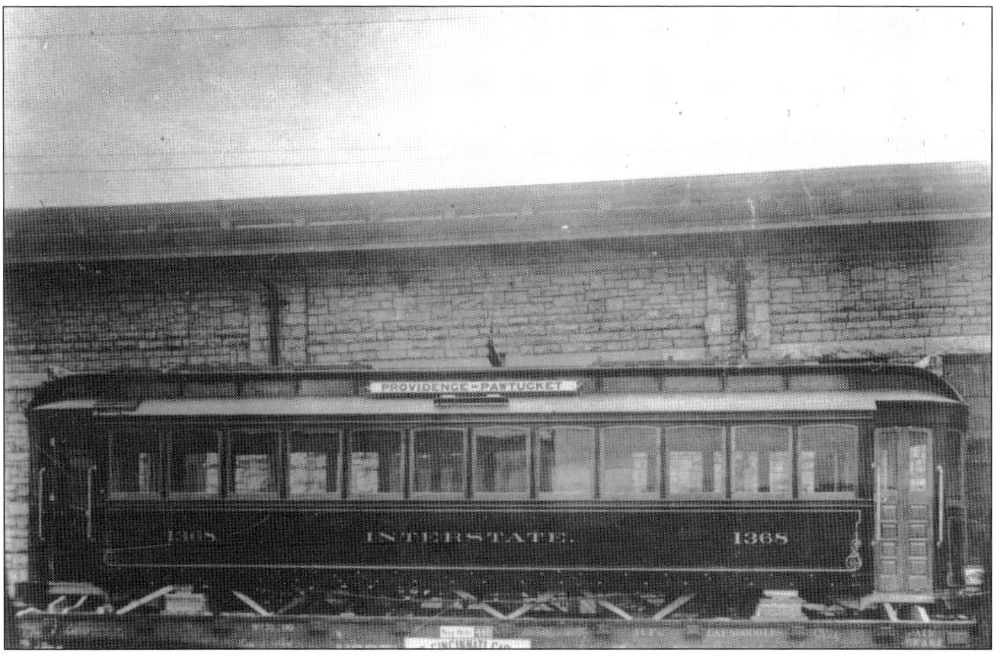

Builder's Photograph, Car No. 1368. Wason Manufacturing Company built railway passenger coaches and streetcars. Wason was located in Springfield, Massachusetts. Many of Rhode Island's early trolley car companies contracted with Wason to build cars for their lines.

Prairie Avenue Line. Prior to 1938, the Prairie Avenue line began its run at Dorrance and Weybosset Streets. The line had many stops along its route, making it convenient for many who shopped in Providence.

Car No. 1699, Gansett Avenue. Trolley car No. 1699 was 29 feet long and weighed 16,715 pounds. It had 22 wooden seats and was built in 1922.

Three

CAR HOUSES

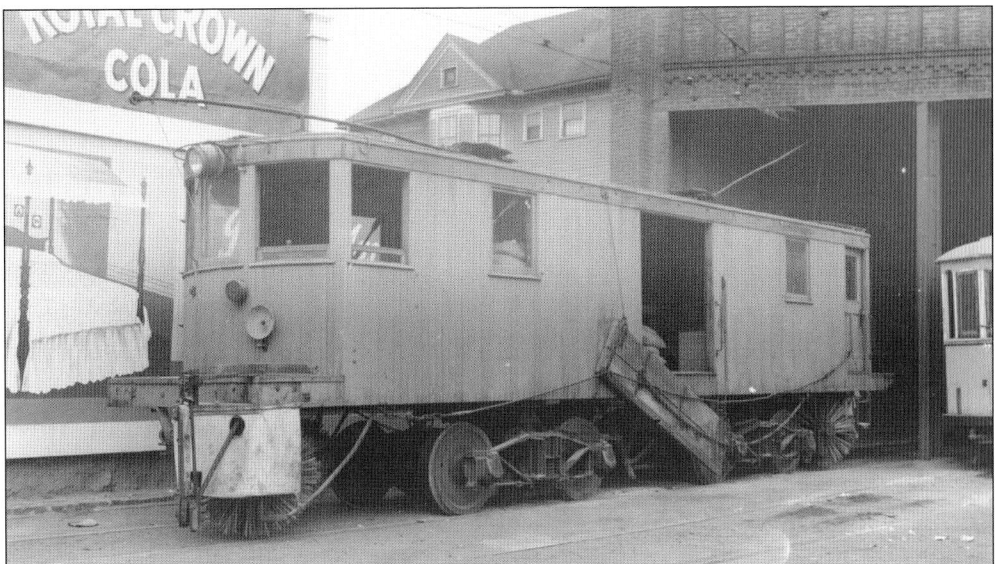

SWEEPER CAR, BROAD STREET CAR HOUSE. Removing snow from trolley tracks was a vital part of keeping the cars on schedule. Sweeper cars had rotary brooms powered by electric motors. These brooms worked well in brushing the snow and ice off the tracks.

Broad Street Car House. United Electric Railways owned many trolley car houses, also called car barns, throughout the state. Many of the larger car houses had clock towers. These large clocks were of great help in keeping the trolley cars on schedule.

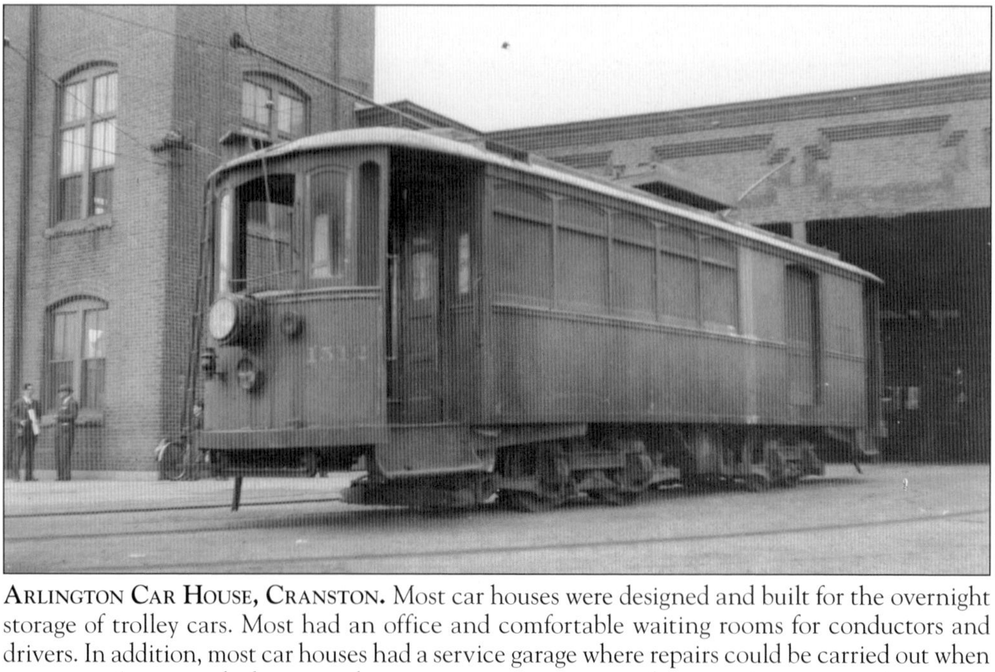

Arlington Car House, Cranston. Most car houses were designed and built for the overnight storage of trolley cars. Most had an office and comfortable waiting rooms for conductors and drivers. In addition, most car houses had a service garage where repairs could be carried out when necessary. At one end of most car houses was a storage room where repair parts were kept.

SWEEPER CAR, BROAD STREET CAR HOUSE (ABOVE) AND THURBERS AVENUE CAR HOUSE (BELOW). The Thurbers Avenue car house was located at the intersection of Thurbers Avenue and Broad Street in Providence, close to the Cranston city line. The building fronted Thurbers Avenue and housed dozens of trolley cars that served the transportation needs of many in Providence and Cranston. The trolley lines and tracks came out of the building at Broad Street on one end and Prairie Avenue at the other end.

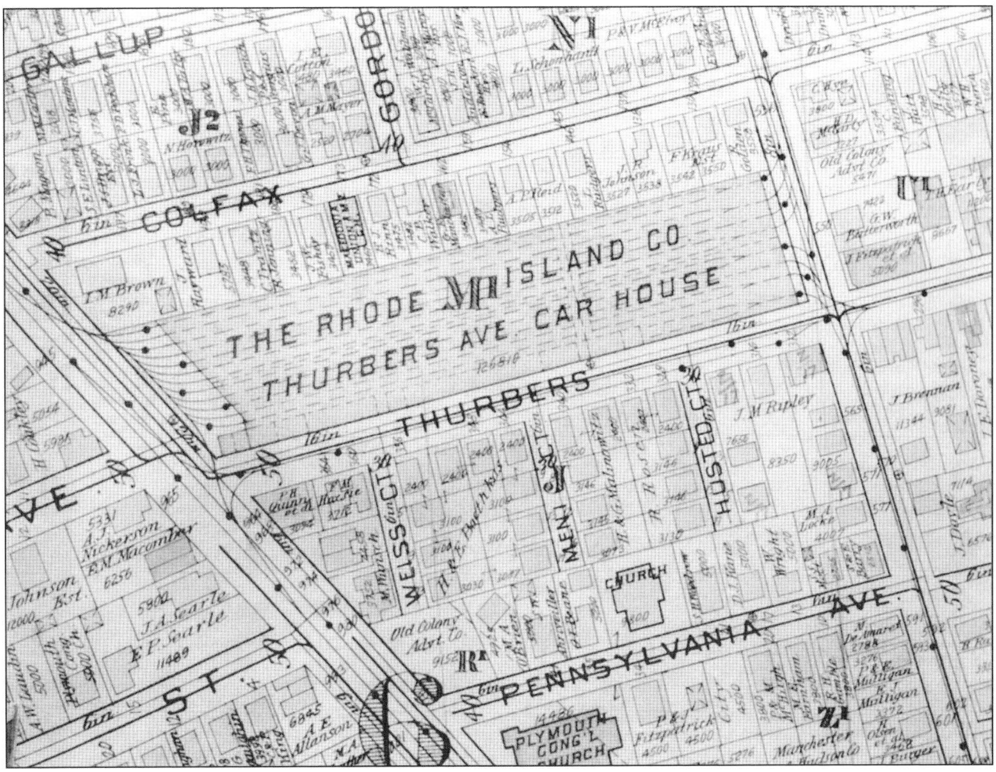

ACADEMY AVENUE CAR HOUSE. The Academy Avenue car house was located on Academy Avenue in Providence.

CAR NO. 1565, CRANSTON CAR HOUSE. At the beginning of 1902, a street-sprinkling system was implemented in Providence to help control dust. About 20 miles of street were sprinkled (watered) daily. The company had three sprinkling trolley cars, each with the capacity to carry 2,400 gallons of water, that were used to accomplish the sprinkling throughout the city.

North Main Street Car House with Car in Front. The North Main Street car house was located on North Main Street in Providence close to the Providence-Pawtucket city line. The North Main Street car house closed to active service on April 21, 1939.

North Main Street Car House. Prior to 1895, there were car barns for horse-drawn cars in Providence and surrounding cities and towns. The larger car barns were located at Elmwood Avenue, Cranston, Olneyville, Manton, Mount Pleasant, Branch Avenue, and Pidge Avenue. Most of these car barns were built to accommodate horse-drawn cars; after 1895, many of these car barns were sold or abandoned, and new car houses were built to accommodate electric trolley cars.

ELMWOOD CAR HOUSE. The Elmwood Avenue car house was located on Elmwood Avenue in Providence. Built by the Rhode Island Company, the building was constructed of brick with a distinctive pier-and-panel wall motif. It was put in service in 1902. The building was 360 feet long and 200 feet wide, with 14 tracks that entered the building. The building could house 126 trolley cars.

ELMWOOD AVENUE GARAGE. In later years, the Elmwood Avenue car house was referred to as the Elmwood Avenue Garage, from which a large number of the Rhode Island Company's trackless trolley buses were dispatched.

Prairie Avenue Car House. The Prairie Avenue car house was located on the west side of Prairie Avenue at its intersection with Thurbers Avenue. It was built around 1900 for the storage and service of trolley cars for the Union Railroad Company. This building replaced an older structure that was used to store horsecars. This new building was designed for larger electrified trolley cars.

Olneyville Car House. The Olneyville Car House was located on Hartford Avenue in Providence. The majority of the early open-type trolley cars from the Olneyville line were painted dark green. These cars were later replaced, and by 1920, they were all enclosed-type cars.

Interior, Cranston Street Car House. The Cranston Street Car House was also referred to as Arlington. Arlington was a neighborhood (village) in Cranston. The Cranston Street Car House had a pit between the tracks that allowed the undercarriage of the car to be easily inspected and serviced daily.

Plow No. 15 at Cranston Street Car House. Trolley car companies were required to keep their tracks clear of snow and in a safe condition. Snowplow cars could effectively push snow from the tracks, clearing any buildup of snow and ice.

Trolley Car in Cranston Street Car House. Trolley cars had a large bell mounted under the car. This bell was referred to by many as "the gong." Operated by the motorman's foot, it was used as a warning signal. The gong was a necessity for the motorman when operating in the city and at street crossings.

Near Broad Street Car House. During the life of a trolley car, many cars are renumbered when the ownership of a company changes hands. For example, car No. 1511 started out as Union Railroad car No. 60. It was renumbered 1511 after being put into service as a United Electric Railways car.

Cars Parked in Cranston Car House. In 1893, the Union Railroad Company had about 1,700 horses used to pull cars on the company's 65 miles of track. The Elmwood stable, South Providence stable, and Traverse Street stables were three of the larger facilities.

Four

STATIONS AND STOPS

DUBY'S GROVE JUNCTION, CRANSTON. Along the Buttonwoods line was a place known as Duby's Grove Junction. Many people from the area would come to Duby's Grove for recreational activities and relaxation. Fishing and boating on the Pawtuxet River were popular activities.

ROCKY POINT JUNCTION, BUTTONWOODS LINE. The Buttonwoods line was constructed in 1875 by the Warwick Railroad Company. The line initially went from Oakland Beach on to Buttonwoods. In later years, operations of the line were transferred several times. The Rhode Island Company leased the line and operated it for many years until it was closed in 1935. In 1889, the Buttonwood to Providence line made many stops along a long route. Stations along the

way were named Buttonwoods, Oakland Beach, Warwick, Rocky Point, Grants, Bayside (which later became known as Longmeadows), River View, Shawomet Beach, Conimicut, Cole's, Hoxie, Spring Green, Pawtuxet, Silver Hook, Belfont, Auburn, Roger Williams Park, Elmwood, Cranston Street, Olneyville, and Providence.

Silver Hook Station (above) and Just Past Silver Hook Station (below), c. 1935. Silver Hook Station (later known as Lakewood Station) was located about six miles from Providence. Along this route, Duby's Grove junction was where the line from Providence connected with the Warwick Avenue line. Many children of the area took the trolley from Lakewood Station to attend the Lakewood High School. The school was built in 1925.

Longmeadows Station. Longmeadows junction was a little over a half-mile from Shawomet Station. Along the line was Rocky Point junction, which connected to a short spur track off the main line.

Longmeadows Station, April 1940. The braking system for most trolley cars built after 1900 was operated by compressed air. A large air tank mounted beneath the car was filled with air from an electric air compressor also mounted beneath the car. The compressor cycled on and off, providing around 80 pounds of pressure to the tank. A valve that directed air from the tank to the brake cylinders was operated by the motorman when needed.

WARWICK COVE DRAWBRIDGE (ABOVE) AND WARWICK COVE DRAWBRIDGE TO OAKLAND BEACH (BELOW). Buttonwoods was reached by a trestle across a saltwater cove. Trolley cars going to and coming back from Oakland Beach crossed a swing bridge at Warwick Cove. The Buttonwoods line ran a distance of about 14 miles from Providence; it was electrified in the early 1900s and operated as a trolley line by the Rhode Island Suburban Railway Company. The Rhode Island Company later took control of the line and updated it. The line was double-tracked and had 19 stops along the way.

Shawomet Beach Station. Shawomet Beach Station was a very busy stop, as were other stops along the Buttonwoods line. On the weekends, a large increase in traffic was common. Many in the area would head for the station in the morning to take the trolley to Rocky Point Park. Additional cars were dispatched to meet the influx of passenger traffic at peak hours.

Car No. 680, Palace Garden Station, c. 1933. Trolley car No. 680, pictured at Palace Garden Station, was one of several cars that serviced the Buttonwoods line. Some stations along the Buttonwoods Line were removed from service and others renamed during the span of time when the Buttonwoods line was in operation.

Inbound at Cole's Station. Cole's Station was located along the tracks in the vicinity of the "Coles Farm," a well-known location along the Buttonwoods line.

Roger Williams Park. Trolley car No. 2163 was an express car that ran from North Main Street to Providence and Pawtucket. It made fewer stops than the regular line car. Having fewer stops greatly increased its turnaround time.

Express Car No. 2163. On March 7, 1892, the Union Railroad Company petitioned the Providence City Council for permission to lay track on Broad Street from Roger Williams Park to the city line; the company also requested additional extensions to other lines throughout the city.

Rocky Point Excursion via Eddy Street and at Rocky Point, c. 1931. Excursion trips to Rocky Point Park by trolley car were very popular and a good revenue source for the trolley company. Most of these excursion trips were handled by an express car that only picked up and dropped off passengers at a few locations, greatly improving the car's travel time.

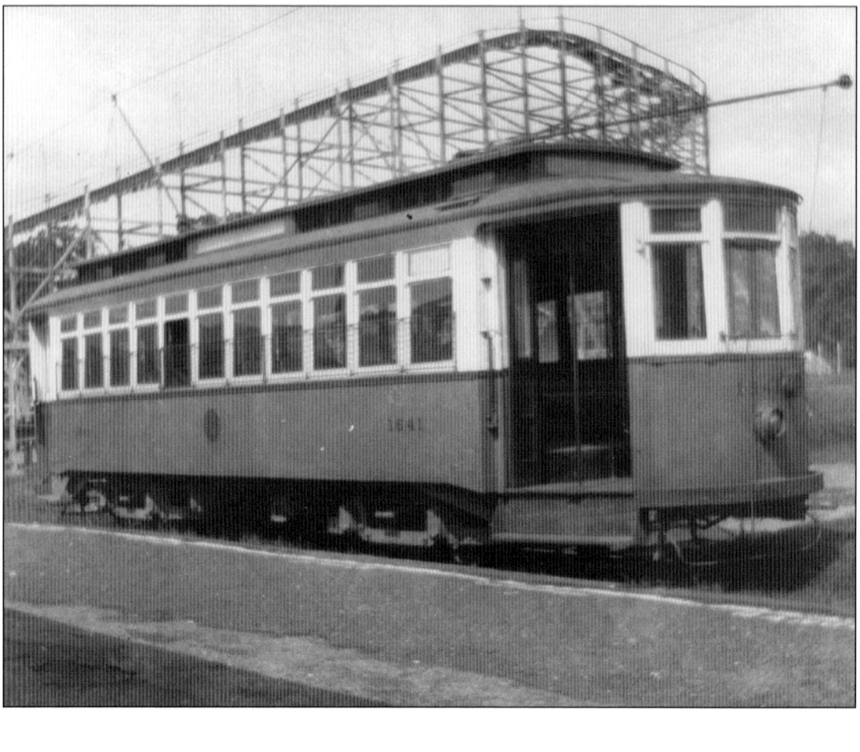

Olneyville Square in Providence (above) and Olneyville Car No. 1107 (below). The Olneyville line began operations in early 1865. In February 1869, the Olneyville line had several horse-drawn trolleys in use, covering several routes. By November, the number increased to 14 horse-drawn trolleys. The average length of a trolley trip was six miles, with trolleys running, on average, every seven and a half minutes and the average number of passengers per car being about 45. The Olneyville line was one of several companies that would later become part of the Union Railroad Company.

Trolley Leaving Swan Point Station (above) and Trolley Car No. 2121 at Swan Point (below). In May 1894, the Rhode Island General Assembly granted a charter for the Swan Point Cemetery, and within a few months, plans were in place for a grand cemetery to be built. In October 1894, provisions were made by the Union Railroad Company to extend its lines to Swan Point.

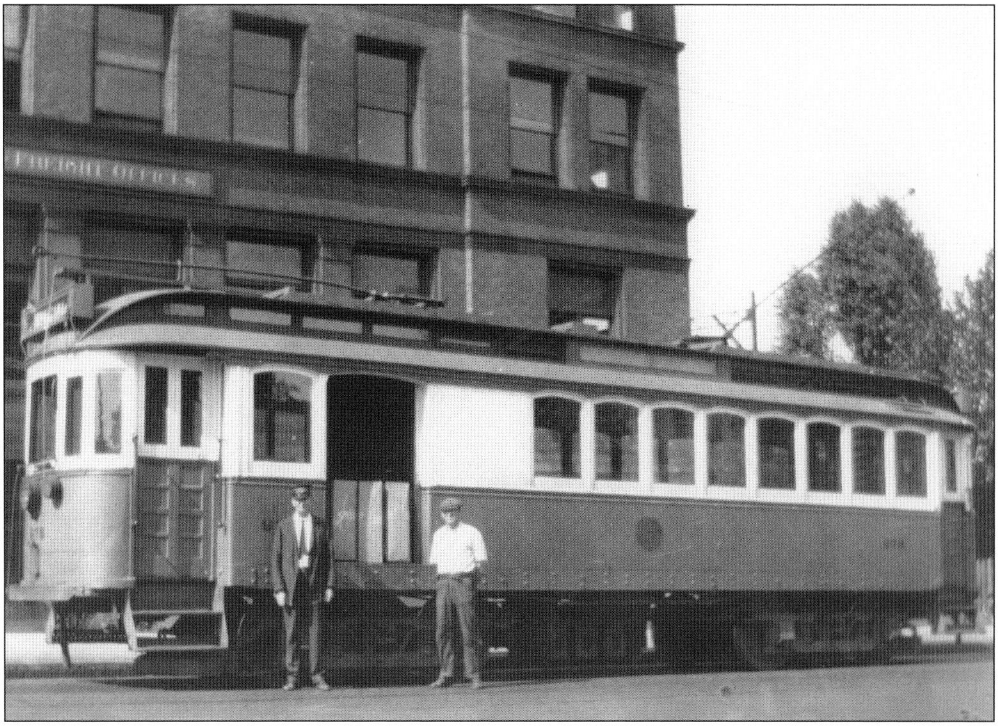

Mail Service Car No. 678. United Electric Railways car No. 678, referred to as the mail car, was used on the Buttonwoods line to transport mail as well as passengers. Many people along the Buttonwoods line depended on the mail car for their mail as well as other merchandise that could be shipped.

No. 1036 on Mineral Spring Avenue. Bad weather would greatly hinder the movement of passengers and freight. This created a backlog, forcing trolley companies to add additional cars to the routes.

Western Entrance to Tunnel, c. 1930 (above), and East Side Entrance to Tunnel, c. 1939 (below). The East Side Trolley Tunnel was built to improve transportation between the East Side and the commercial center of Providence. The tunnel began serving the people of Providence in 1914, and the cost of the project was $700,000. The tunnel ran over 2,000 feet beneath College Hill on Providence's East Side. The west end of the tunnel began at South Main Street, and its east end began at Thayer Street.

HOPE STREET CAR AT ALUMNI AVENUE. Pictured here is the Hope Street car at the Alumni Avenue Turnout in a typical snowstorm snarl of traffic around 1920.

LEAVING EAST SIDE EXIT OF TUNNEL. In 1948, the trolley tracks in the East Side Trolley Tunnel were removed and the tunnel roadbed was paved for the use of trackless trolleys and buses.

UNION STATION (ABOVE) AND A CAR NEAR THE EAST SIDE TUNNEL ENTRANCE (BELOW). Union Station first opened in Providence in 1847; it was built to accommodate the city's fast-growing need for a centralized transportation hub. The station expanded in size over those early years. However, a catastrophic fire heavily damaged the station in February 1896.

Union Station, Providence. After the 1896 fire at Union Station, a new, larger station was planned to handle an ever-increasing demand for city and state transportation needs. In 1898, the new station was completed and put in service. This new station was designed to accommodate the movement of a large number of people coming in to and leaving the state daily. The station was also designed to accommodate trolley car traffic coming and going from the station.

SCHOOL CAR ON THE BUTTONWOODS LINE (ABOVE) AND BUTTONWOODS CAR NO. 678 (BELOW). The Rhode Island Company Seaview Division sold school tickets or commutation tickets, as did many other lines, at its ticket stations. It was suggested that these tickets should be purchased three days before the first ride is to be taken. They were round-trip tickets issued to pupils attending school. In 1913, the cost for one month's worth of tickets (60 rides total) on the Narragansett division lines was about $3.15.

Five

Improving the Tracks

Empire Street, Providence, c. 1941. The maintenance and upkeep of the many miles of trolley wire and tracks presented a daunting job for track crews. Within the provisions agreed upon by the railway companies, repairs and maintenance of track were required by law. In addition to keeping the lines and intersection in good condition, the railway companies also required the removal of snow. During the winter months, track crews struggled to keep the many miles of track in a safe condition.

Chalkstone and Mount Pleasant Avenues (above) and Exchange Place (below), Providence. Snowplows were essential in keeping the track clear of snow so trolley cars could pass during bad weather. The crews of the plow cars were specially trained to deal with various snow conditions. In the early years of the electric railways, many snowplow cars were open, leaving the crew exposed to the weather. By 1899, most of the plow cars were redesigned and had a closed body, greatly improving the operation of the snowplow cars. In the winter of 1890, Rhode Island trolley companies had over 25 plow cars in operation.

Plow on Cranston Street. During extreme cold snaps, thick blankets of ice would form around the tracks, causing trolley cars to derail. Many different methods of removing the ice were tried. Many companies relied on pick-and-shovel gangs to break up the ice. The pick and- shovel gangs would normally be followed by a sweeper car. This method was slow, but the results were good. On occasion, gasoline was used to melt thick ice on the roadbed. The gasoline would be sprinkled along the rails and then ignited. This was effective but had its limitations. Snow fences were used along many lines to prevent blowing snow from building up along the tracks.

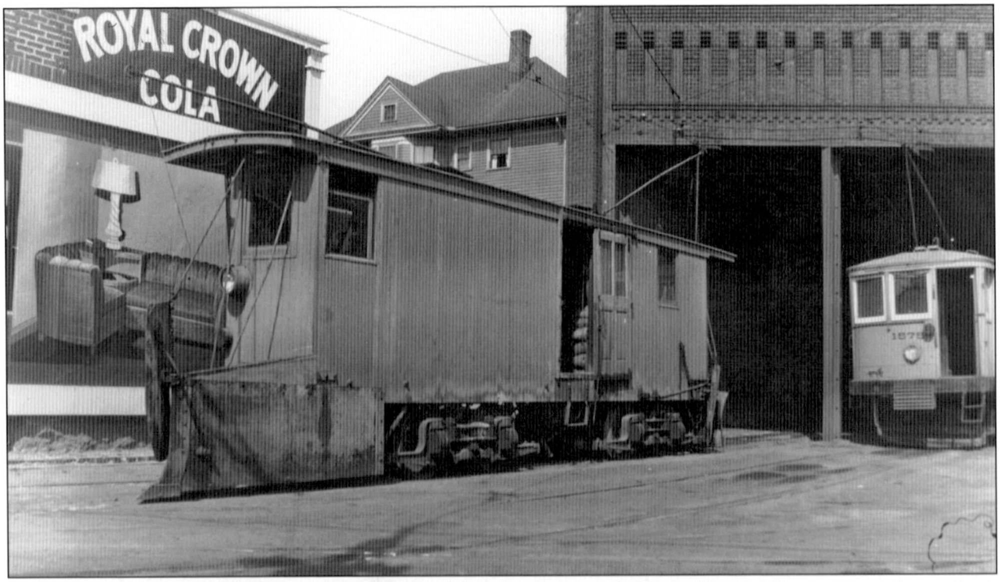

BROAD STREET CAR HOUSE, C. 1946. Trolley companies purchased snowplow cars to keep their tracks clear in the winter. Many of these utility cars were purchased from the Wason Manufacturing Company of Springfield, Massachusetts.

NORTH MAIN STREET, C. 1938. Car No. 9 was referred to as a utility car. This plow car had what was called a "wedge plow" mounted on the front of the car. It also had two small wing plows on each side.

PLOW NO. 74, FRANKLIN STREET (ABOVE), AND PLOW NO. 15, CRANSTON STREET (BELOW). Woonsocket was one of the first lines to embrace electrification. In 1888, the Woonsocket Electric Machine & Power Company began building the equipment needed to replace a few old horsecars with electric trolley cars. The benefit was quickly realized, and within a short time, all the remaining cars were electrified. Following the success of the Woonsocket line, Newport began to electrify its cars. The dependability of the new electric cars, along with the more comfortable and safer ride, brought many skeptics of the electric car around. Within a few years, the race was on for electrification.

SWEEPER, NORTH MAIN STREET (ABOVE), AND SWEEPER NO. 109 (BELOW), C. 1941. Sweeper cars were used to remove snow and keep tracks clear. Trolley plows and sweepers were kept busy clearing track as snow was falling. During a large snowfall, plow cars and sweepers could only push the snow to one side of the track; this caused many problems after a large snowstorm.

CRANE CAR, CRANSTON STREET (ABOVE), AND CRANE CAR PULLING UP RAILS (BELOW). By the time United Electric Railways took control of most of Rhode Island's electric railway service, a vast variety of service equipment was in use. Many service cars were specifically built for laying and removing track. A large number of these service cars were constructed from old passenger cars or obsolete freight cars no longer adequate for their intended use.

Crane Car Laying New Track (above) and Crane (below), East Providence. A crane car was a flatcar that had a pillar-type crane mounted on one side. The crane was used to move rails and other heavy objects. The crane car was a critical piece of equipment used for keeping the tracks in good order. The crane car was also used to clear wreckage from a derailment or accident.

New Track by Biltmore Hotel (above) and Track-Laying Crew (below). Track-laying crews worked throughout the year in all types of weather. When the crews were laying track in the city, many onlookers would gather to admire the skill and hard work it took to perform this task.

Crane Car (above) and Men Working (Left) on the Trestle at Duby's Grove. Pictured is United Electric Railways crane car No. 1536 with its crew at work strengthening the trestle bridges at Duby's Grove in the fall of 1941. Trestle bridges were constantly inspected, and keeping them in a safe condition kept track crews busy throughout the year.

CRANE TRUCK NO. 123 (ABOVE) AND TRACK SERVICE CAR (BELOW). As rubber-tired motorized trucks began replacing horses and wagons as utility vehicles, their reliability and versatility became apparent. United Electric Railways crane truck No. 123 was one of the first rubber-tired motorized trucks used by the company. It could be quickly dispatched to a trolley line problem or to assist with a trolley that had broken down.

NEW TRACK AT CITY HALL. Track crews were kept busy maintaining, replacing, or laying new track. Much planning went into the construction of a new trolley line or the extension of an existing line.

NEW TRACK, BROAD STREET LOOP. When new track was laid, the work was carried out as quickly as possible in an effort to keep the inconvenience to the public at a minimum.

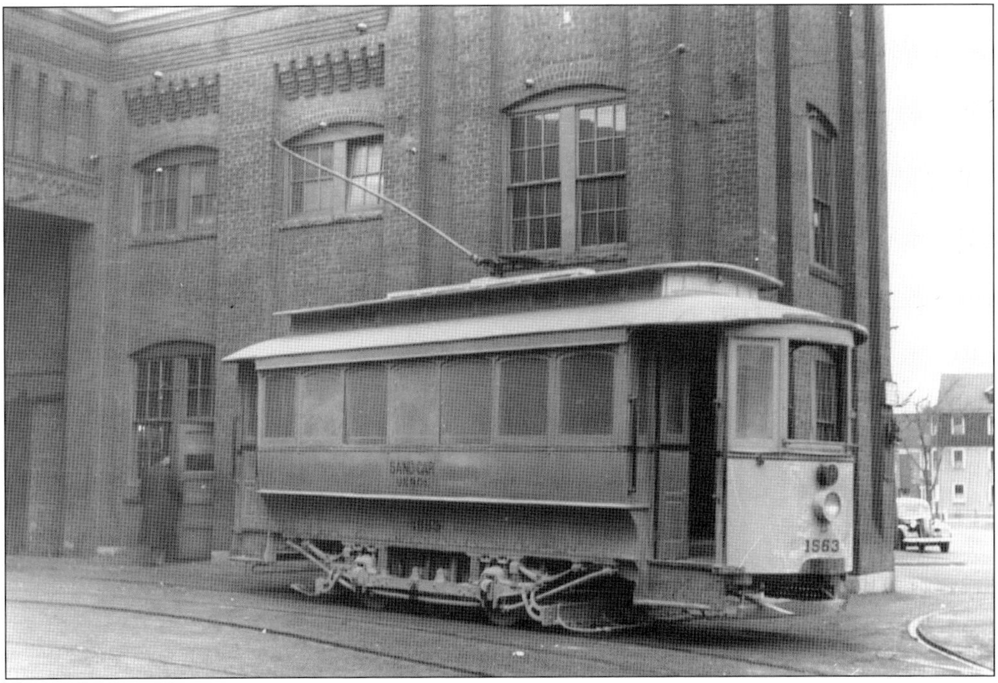

Sand Cars Nos. 1563 (above) and 1567 (below). United Electric Railways sand car No. 1563 was used to dispense sand onto the tracks; this was done to increase the traction on slippery rails. This was especially important at intersections and steep hills. Many accidents occurred when a car was unable to stop due to a lack of traction.

Service Car No. 1515 (above) and Training Snowplow Crew (below). Snowplow crews were trained in removing snow and ice from track and trolley wires. Training beforehand on the proper operation of a snowplow car was extremely important. Many relied on snow crews to keep the tracks clear and in a safe condition. The difficulty of seeing what was on the tracks during a heavy snowfall was one of the biggest obstacles for a plow operator.

Emergency Car at Broad Street Car House. The Broad Street car house served as the dispatch location for United Electric Railways emergency vehicles. UER emergency car No. 1504 was used when a trolley car had a mechanical breakdown or other such emergency.

Service Car No. 1529. The emergency car, as it was called, was equipped with the tools to quickly repair a disabled car and also carried many spare parts needed for an on-the-spot repair. If a disabled car could not be repaired on the spot, the emergency car was equipped to move the disabled car to the company's repair shop.

UNITED ELECTRIC RAILWAYS TRACK MEN (LEFT) AND GEORGE M. COHAN BOULEVARD (BELOW). George M. Cohan was a beloved American entertainer born in Providence in 1878. Beginning as a child performer at the age of eight, Cohan and his family members toured extensively while performing various vaudeville shows. He was greatly admired throughout the state for his many talents. Cohan passed away on November 5, 1942. Deeply missed by many in Rhode Island, he was memorialized throughout the state.

EDGEWOOD VIA EDDY STREET. From the beginning of the horse-drawn trolley to the era of electrification, safety was a paramount concern. Accidents came in many forms. Trolleys striking pedestrians was a major problem for many trolley companies. One early pedestrian safety device was the "pedestrian catcher," or people catcher, as they were called. This was a device that was installed on some early trolley cars. It was designed to drop down onto the rails and scoop up an unfortunate pedestrian that had fallen in front of a moving car. The car shown here derailed due to a collapse of the roadbed.

Car No. 1052 Destroyed by Fire (above) and Providence Car, Chepachet (below). Under a charter granted to the Providence & Danielson Railway by the state of Rhode Island, the Rhode Island Company began construction of the Chepachet line in the fall of 1913. After much work, the line was completed in July 1914. The line was about 16 miles long and was typical of most New England trolley routes.

UNITED ELECTRIC RAILWAYS CRANE CAR OVERTURNS (ABOVE) AND CRANSTON REPAIR YARD (BELOW). The trackless trolley fleet of the United Electric Railways Company was made up of vehicles made by several different manufacturers, with one being the Pullman company. The Pullman trackless trolley bus was well made, but some of the first buses the company built had some design problems, with one being that it was hard to steer. Many drivers complained, and the vehicles were taken out of service until the problem was corrected by the manufacturer. In addition to the difficult steering, the valve that controlled the air to the horn would occasionally freeze open in cold weather. When this happened on a busy route, it caused extreme havoc all along the line.

Replacing Track (above) and Hoyle Square, Providence (below). A spur track that went to Rocky Point came off the Buttonwoods line. Throughout the state, a trip to Rocky Point during the summer months was an annual tradition. Many loved a scenic trolley ride on the Buttonwoods line in an open car, stopping at every station along the way.

Electric Locomotive Being Built. Referred to as electric locomotives or engine cars, these powerful locomotives were used for pulling freight cars or trains.

Engine Car No. 1297. The Rhode Island Company built three electric locomotives to handle freight traffic along its lines. The three locomotives, or engines, as they were called, were numbered 1295, 1296, and 1297. These three engines were built between 1904 and 1911. All three were 29 feet and 8 inches long with 4/Wh 93 electric motors.

Moving Freight Car over Trestle (above) and Car No. 1511 (below). These electric locomotives were vital in the day-to-day movement of freight cars along the line. Most trolley companies transported freight along their lines; in most cases, the trolley company depended on the revenue generated by this service.

UNITED ELECTRIC RAILWAYS LOCOMOTIVE PULLING COAL CARS (ABOVE) AND SERVICE CARS AT CRANSTON STREET CAR HOUSE (BELOW). Many trolley routes transported both passengers and freight. Many of the early trolley freight cars were built or modified from old horsecars. Over time and with an ever-increasing demand to move products and goods throughout Rhode Island, freight cars were specifically purchased to meet that demand. Most freight arrived at outbound warehouses or stations, then the shipment would immediately be routed to the appropriate car. During United Electric Railways' busiest years, the freight department had over 80 freight cars and 3 electric locomotives in service. As the freight business declined, several of these freight cars were refitted for work as service cars.

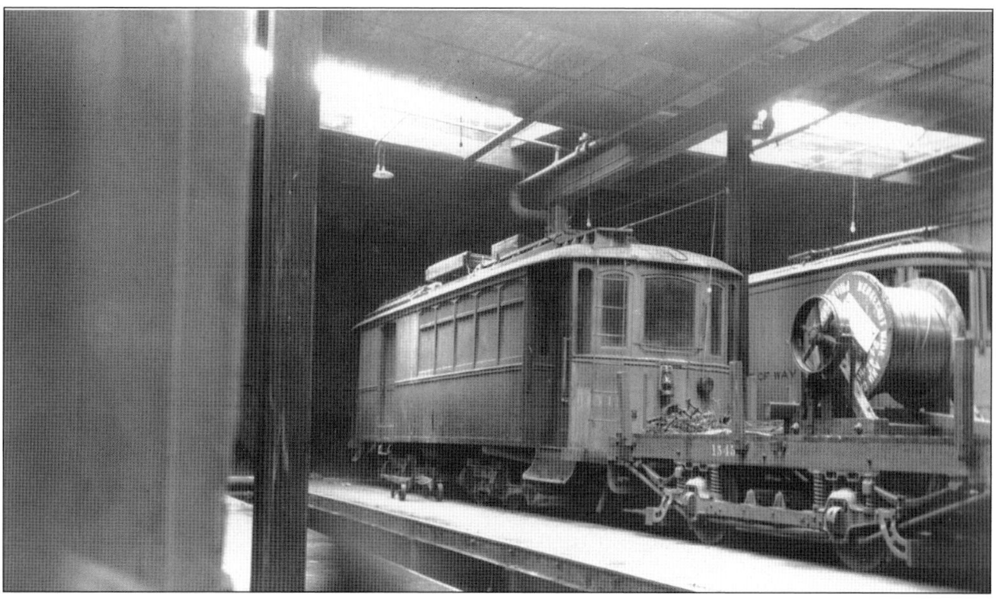

Scrap Line Fire (above) and United Electric Railways Car No. 1049, Pawtucket (below). Many early trolley cars were open to the weather, making the unfortunate passengers endure freezing weather during the winter months. A trolley car traveling over uneven track would, over time, begin to creak and rattle. These "rattletrap cars," as they were sometimes called, would be taken out of service. Many of the cars were repurposed for uses other than transporting passengers or scrapped.

BELLEFONTE MOVING FREIGHT (ABOVE) AND MOUNT PLEASANT LINE (BELOW). From 1910 to the end of World War II, the shipping of freight brought the Rhode Island Company and its successor, United Electric Railways, large profits. The revenue from the freight business enabled the company to expand service and buy new equipment when needed. In 1913, between 90 and 100 carloads of freight traveled in and out of the Providence freight station daily. Also that year, the old power station on Eddy Street was remodeled and converted into an efficient freight-handling station.

PAY CAR ON SCRAP LINE (ABOVE) AND PAY CAR AT HOYLE SQUARE, PROVIDENCE (BELOW). Most trolley companies would have a pay car in service that would deliver pay envelopes to company employees each week. Both the company and employees found this to be a convenient way of receiving their wages.

Rhode Island Company Power Station (Right) and United Electric Railways Line Crew (below). The vast network of trolley power lines carried a 600-volt direct current (DC). In 1920, the average operational life expectancy of a new electric trolley car was about 17 years. Early electric trolley cars were powered by 25-horsepower electric motors. The car's operator engaged the motors from a controller that sent power to the motors. There was a deadman safety handle on the controller in case the operator became incapacitated.

Rail Puller Car, c. 1939. Motor flatcars are used to carry freight and other large items. These types of cars are self-propelled flatcars powered by electricity.

Buttonwoods Line Track Car. Motor flatcars were modified and used as utility cars. These cars were used in maintaining and replacing the track when needed.

Overhead Wires, Arlington Car House (Right) and Old Cranston Car House, Webster Avenue (below). Trolley wire carried the current needed to power the trolley cars. Overhead repairs and maintenance of the many miles of trolley wire presented a daunting task for maintenance crews. On occasion, a main trolley wire would break during rush hour, which resulted in a large number of cars being delayed. This would severely disrupt the schedule, leaving many disgruntled patrons waiting for service to resume.

Frances Street, Providence (above) and Car No. 101 on Scrap Line (below). Trolley wire was mostly made up of copper and needed to be maintained and replaced from time to time due to wear. The diameter of the wire and the number of cars operating under the wire determined its usable lifespan. Much planning took place prior to installing new trolley wire. Proper installation was of paramount importance to safeguard the protection of the public and the linemen that serviced the wire.

Six

LOVE THY TROLLEY

HOME BUILT FROM TROLLEY CARS. Obsolete equipment was a constant concern for many railway companies. After the usable life of a trolley was determined, the car would be taken and placed on what was called a scrap line, where the usable parts could be salvaged. The body of a decommissioned trolley car would sometimes be repurposed or sold as scrap. Pictured is a home in Oakland Beach built around two trolley car bodies. The cars were numbered 1704 and 1705.

Buttonwoods Car Leaving Providence (above) and Car No. 2114 and Driver (left). Each day, a trolley would leave Exchange Place in Providence every 30 minutes for the trip to Buttonwoods. The round trip took two hours and cost 15¢. A trip to Oakland Beach and Buttonwoods was highly recommended for those vacationing in Rhode Island.

Prairie Avenue Shop (above) and Elmwood Garage (below). The Cranston Repair Shop was a large facility on Cranston Street that was fully equipped to handle all phases of streetcar maintenance and repair. In addition to routine repairs, the facility routinely overhauled and updated cars that had seen a lot of service. During the conversion to a trackless trolley system, United Electric Railways decided to close the Cranston repair shop and relocate repair service to an updated shop located in the Prairie Avenue end of the Broad Street car house. In Providence, several routes were selected as test routes for trackless trolley service. In the early part of 1935, the overhead lines that powered the trackless trolleys were put in place, and on June 23, 1935, a test of this new type of trolley bus went into service. The Elmwood Garage was located at Elmwood Avenue and Russell Street.

SERVICE CAR, COLLEGE HILL (LEFT) AND BROAD STREET CAR HOUSE (BELOW). The Providence Cable Tramway Company built a cable line up College Street in Providence in 1889. The cable line went up College Street through Waterman Street to East River Street and then returned by way of South Angell and Prospect Streets to College Street. The Union Railroad purchased most of the stock of the Providence Cable Tramway Company in 1891 and continued operating cable cars along this line.

COLLEGE HILL, PROVIDENCE (RIGHT) AND APPROACHING COLLEGE HILL (BELOW). A grip car such as the one that ran up College Hill in Providence had a clutching device attached to the front of the car that would grip the cable that ran beneath the surface of the street. Once the car gripped onto the cable, the clutching device would pull the car along and up the hill.

NORTH MAIN STREET CAR HOUSE (ABOVE) AND CARS OUT OF SERVICE (BELOW). In the 1870s, a horsecar line was built from Apponaug to Buttonwoods. In 1881, the Warwick Railroad was extended to Buttonwoods, providing a direct connection from Providence. This made it possible for more people to enjoy the Warwick Shore and the fine camping at Buttonwoods. It was, in part, the transformation from steam to electric in the early part of the 1900s that made the development of Buttonwoods possible.

The Washington Bridge and Main Street (above) and Pawtucket Avenue, Providence (below). The Washington Bridge along Route 195 in Providence was built in 1930, replacing an older bridge at that site. It was constructed using reinforced concrete with 12 granite-faced spans.

Fields Point Shipyard (above) and a Car Heading down Thurbers Avenue (below). Fields Point was named after Thomas Field, a British colonist who settled the site in the 17th century. At the beginning of World War II, the US Maritime Commission chose Fields Point as a site for the construction of a shipyard under the Emergency Shipbuilding Program.

No Power, 1938 Hurricane. In 1938, United Electric Railways was moving quickly to modernize its streetcar service and replace them with trackless trolley buses wherever possible. However, the company's efforts were put on hold when a powerful hurricane barreled through Rhode Island and caused tremendous damage throughout the state.

Broad Street Car House, June 1935. The 1938 hurricane caused sufficient damage and halted trolley service for days. Service crews battled to repair the numerous overhead trolley lines brought down by the storm.

Weybosset and Empire Streets (above) and North Main Street (below). Prior to 1928, the paint scheme of many of the trolley cars in Rhode Island greatly varied, with little standardization. After 1928, United Electric Railways adopted a standard design and color scheme for all of its trolley cars. The company decided on yellow and white for its cars, and the company's car painters went to work. The combination of the two colors was applied and modified to fit the different types of trolley cars on the various lines. At that same time, the circular UER monogram was adopted and located on the center body of the cars.

NEWPORT, RHODE ISLAND (ABOVE), AND CRANSTON REPAIR YARD (BELOW). Early on, Newport had a well-established horsecar line despite the lack of support by the city for the viable system. In the summer of 1889, the Newport Street Railway began operating a trolley service between Fall River and Newport that became very popular. The Newport & Providence Railway Company completed work on a new line running between Newport and Bristol. Newport became one of the first towns in the state to electrify its trolley line.

Market Square, Providence. A trackless trolley, also known as an electric bus or trolley bus, is powered by electricity, which runs the electric motors that propel the bus. Two trolley poles extend from the top of the bus and make contact with a pair of parallel electrified overhead wires; these wires were strung all along the route. Trolley poles along the side of the track support the overhead wires.

Providence City Hall. A trolley car, also known as a streetcar, only needs one overhead wire. The track on which the trolley car ran was used to complete the electrical circuit that powered the motors that propelled the car.

Broad Street City Line Stop. At the Broad Street city line, one could catch a trolley to downtown Providence. Once downtown, one could catch a trolley that connected to routes across almost the entire state.

Waiting Station, Exchange Place Loop. Trolley tracks ran throughout downtown Providence. Many would catch the trolley leaving downtown at the Exchange Place Loop "waiting station."

Car No. 148, Buttonwoods Line. United Electric Railways car No. 148 is pictured here in August 1931 at Buttonwoods Station. No. 148 was an open car—these were much preferred by passengers in the summer months.

United Electric Railways Car No. 678, Buttonwoods Station. This image was also taken in the early 1930s. No. 678 was an enclosed car used during the cooler months.

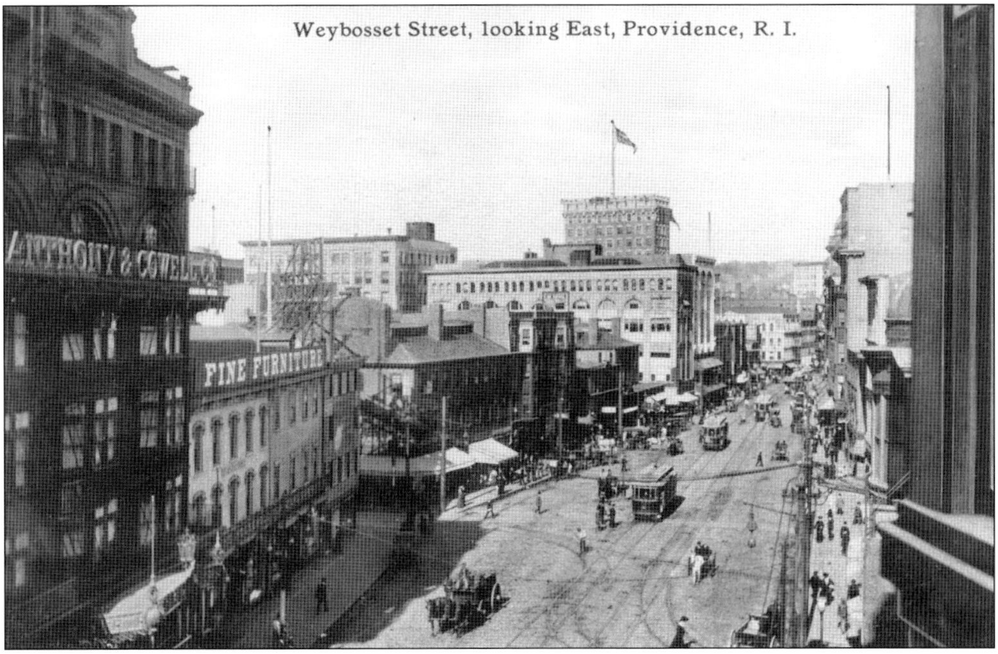

WEYBOSSET STREET, PROVIDENCE (ABOVE), AND DORRANCE STREET ROUTE (BELOW). The Great Depression caused financial hardship for United Electric Railways, as it did with many other electric and steam railway companies. For UER, 1929 became the last year the company paid its shareholders a dividend throughout the Depression years. To reduce costs, the company scaled back the number of streetcars and buses operating on numerous routes.

Broad Street Car House (above) and Providence Car, Newport (below). United Electric Railways car No. 2108 was the last car to enter the Broad Street car house. Trolley service in Providence came to an end, and No. 2108 made its last run, in the early morning hours of Saturday, May 15, 1948. Trolley service in Providence came to an end due to a decrease in ridership and a decline in revenue. In 1952, United Electric Railways was taken over by the United Transit Company. Many in the city were deeply saddened. Most everyone had fond memories of riding the trolley to the beaches or taking a scenic trolley ride on the Buttonwoods line to Rocky Point in the summer months.

Seven

THE TRACKLESS TROLLEY AND RIPTA

EXCHANGE PLACE, C. 1943. Around 1935, United Electric Railways began converting many of its lines in Providence from conventional rail or track-type trolley cars to trackless trolley cars. The trackless trolley was well received when it was first conceived for use in Rhode Island. Many other trolley companies across the United States had already converted to this new form of trolley configuration and found it to be a great improvement over the track-type system. Over the next few years, almost all the lines were converted. It was also at this time that the company began adding buses to many of its routes.

NEW TRACKLESS TROLLEYS (ABOVE) AND TRACKLESS TROLLEYS ARRIVE BY TRAIN (BELOW). In mid-May 1948, the complete transition from a rail system to a rubber-tired system was achieved. The improvements in gasoline bus design made by manufacturers made it a more reliable vehicle for public transportation. By 1949, United Electric Railways had half of its routes serviced by gasoline-powered motor buses and half by trackless trolley buses.

UNLOADING TRACKLESS TROLLEY BUSES. At its pinnacle, the Rhode Island Company had one of the largest traction systems in the United States. The system had as many as 1,000 cars and over 320 miles of track.

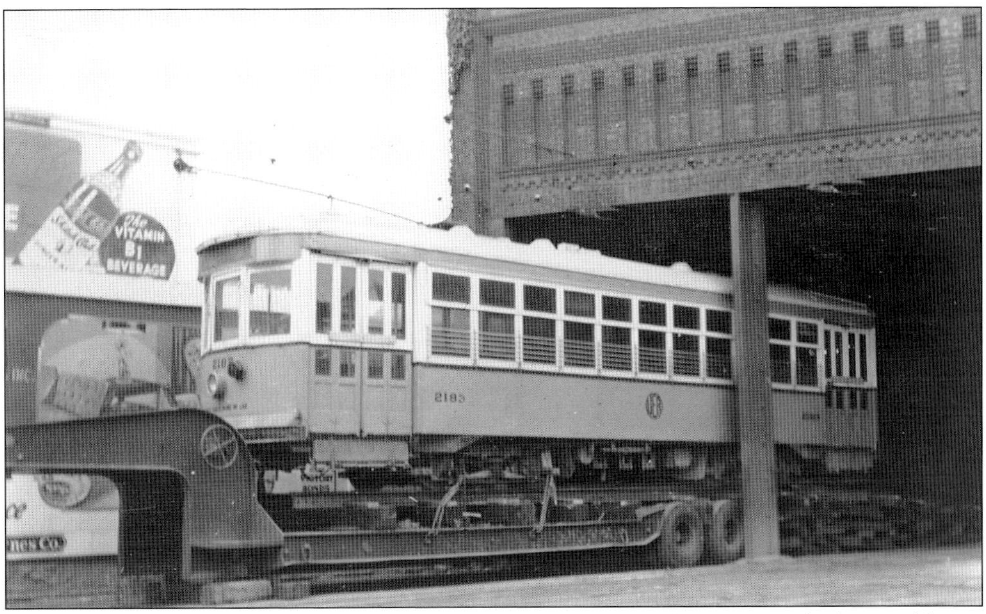

TROLLEY BEING LOADED, BROAD STREET. By 1954, electrified trolleys were in decline and being replaced with gasoline-powered buses.

WAITING ROOM, RHODES ON THE PAWTUXET (ABOVE), AND RHODES ON THE PAWTUXET (BELOW). Gasoline-powered buses operated alongside trackless trolleys on many United Electric Railways routes. The company operated gasoline-powered buses on routes with minimal traffic, while trackless trolleys handled the routes with heavier traffic.

United Electric Railways Bus No. 101 (above) and Melrose Garage (below). The motor bus began showing up in Rhode Island in the early 1920s. There was much skepticism of this new form of transportation and its usefulness in serving the public. Across the United States, several motor bus manufacturing companies began building different types of buses for different classes of service.

WASHING A BUS IN ELMWOOD GARAGE (ABOVE) AND PARK SQUARE GARAGE, WOONSOCKET (BELOW). The motorized bus became the new form of mass transportation, and several aspects of building buses were prioritized. At the top of the list were reliability and customer comfort. The average speed of a bus in the early 1920s was 10 miles per hour, with an operating cost of 28¢ per mile.

MELROSE GARAGE, C. 1928 (ABOVE), AND YELLOW COACH, C. 1926 (BELOW). Over time, the usefulness of the motor bus became apparent. Due to economic conditions, trolley lines in many towns and cities in Rhode Island had become unprofitable. A solution was to incorporate the gasoline-powered bus into many of the company's routes. Its flexibility and lower operating cost made the bus a successful method of transportation in Rhode Island.

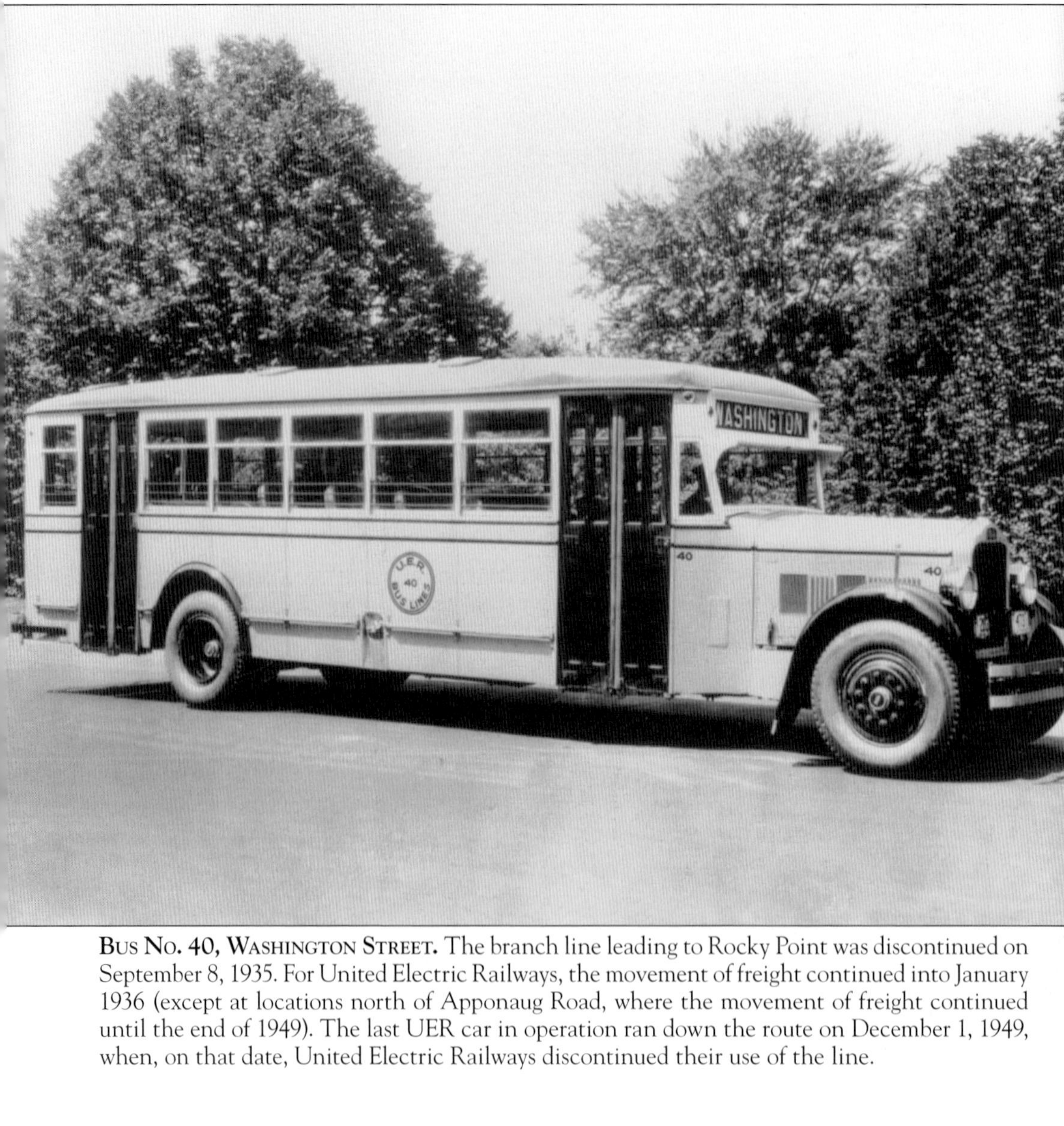

Bus No. 40, Washington Street. The branch line leading to Rocky Point was discontinued on September 8, 1935. For United Electric Railways, the movement of freight continued into January 1936 (except at locations north of Apponaug Road, where the movement of freight continued until the end of 1949). The last UER car in operation ran down the route on December 1, 1949, when, on that date, United Electric Railways discontinued their use of the line.

ELMWOOD GARAGE LOT (ABOVE) AND EXCHANGE PLACE (BELOW), C. 1943. Many of the United Electric Railways Company's trackless trolley lines began operating in early 1930, with the trackless trolleys replacing the steel-wheeled trolley cars that ran on track. Trackless trolley cars had rubber tires and did not need a track on which to ride. However, these trackless trolleys were powered by electric motors and still needed to draw electricity from overhead lines.

Chestnut Hill Avenue Terminal. As operating costs and other factors involved in the operation of trackless trolleys increased, drastic decisions were made, and in the early years of the 1950s, United Electric Railways trackless trolley lines began to close. The Eddy Street trackless trolley line, which began operations on December 30, 1939, was closed on April 9, 1954, along with several other popular routes in the city.

CRANSTON-LINWOOD AVENUE (ABOVE) AND PARKS SQUARE GARAGE, WOONSOCKET (BELOW). Pictured above is United Electric Railways bus No. 242 on its first trip of operation on the Cranston-Linwood Avenue route. Gasoline-powered bus service replaced the trackless trolley on the Cranston-Linwood Avenue route on March 16, 1946.

EXCHANGE PLACE (ABOVE) AND PARKS SQUARE GARAGE (BELOW). The United Electric Railways trackless trolley fleet was housed at two garages. The first was the Pawtucket Garage, which was located near the intersection of Main Street and Lonsdale Avenue. The second was the Elmwood Garage, which was located at Elmwood Avenue and Russell Street in Providence.

APPROACHING EAST STREET TUNNEL. The Elmwood Garage was updated several times. During the conversion to a trackless trolley system, the overhead wiring was updated and reconfigured at the garage to allow for more efficient movement of vehicles in and out of the yard and garage.

UNITED ELECTRIC RAILWAYS BUS NO. 700 (ABOVE) AND UER AIRPORT SERVICE BUS (BELOW). At the Pawtucket Garage, modifications were made in order to accommodate trackless trolleys entering and exiting the garage. Several traffic patterns were tried for buses entering and exiting the yard. A bus wash house was built in 1948, and it was well received by the drivers and repair crews.

DOWNTOWN PROVIDENCE. During World War II, gas rationing forced many to utilize public transportation. The dramatic increase in ridership during the war years brought hope to the trolley companies and their investors, who had seen a decline in ridership prior to the war.

No. 1813 (above) and No. 3812 (below) at Elmwood Garage. Advertising panels adorned the interiors and/or exteriors of most trolley cars and buses. These advertising panels provided a distraction for passengers and a source of income for the company.

New Buses of RIPTA. The Rhode Island Public Transit Authority (RIPTA) was created in 1964 by the Rhode Island General Assembly. RIPTA adopted a policy of upgrading to newer buses and retiring vehicles that outlived their mechanical lives, which became essential in pursuing a quality mass transit system for the state. From the time of its formation, RIPTA set out to increase the accessibility of public transportation for Rhode Island residents, and with this plan came an increase in annual ridership.